the trick of staying and leaving

the trick of staying and leaving

david zieroth

HARBOUR
PUBLISHING

Harbour Publishing Co. Ltd.
P.O. Box 219, Madeira Park, BC, VON 2HO
www.harbourpublishing.com

Edited by Artie Goshulak
Cover design by Libris Simas Ferraz / Onça Publishing
Cover photograph by David Zieroth
Text design by Carleton Wilson
Printed and bound in Canada
Printed on 100% recycled paper

Harbour Publishing acknowledges the support of the Canada Council for the Arts, the Government of Canada, and the Province of British Columbia through the BC Arts Council.

Cataloguing data available from Library and Archives Canada

Title: The trick of staying and leaving / David Zieroth.
Names: Zieroth, David, 1946- author.
Description: Poems.
Identifiers: Canadiana (print) 20220469849 | Canadiana (ebook) 20220469857 | ISBN 9781990776021 (softcover) | ISBN 9781990776038 (EPUB)
Classification: LCC PS8599.I47 T75 2023 | DDC C811/.54—dc23

For Miro

In memory of Dedo (Ernest Dlhoš 1941–2022)

'As I listened to the muffled vowels of the Slovaks and the traffic-jams of consonants and the explosive spurts of dentals and sibilants, my mind's eye automatically suspended an imaginary backcloth of the Slav heartlands behind the speakers…'
— from *A Time of Gifts* by Patrick Leigh Fermor

'Friendship is a sheltering tree.'
— Samuel Taylor Coleridge

contents

Part 1: Arriving

Part 2: Staying

Part 3: Leaving

Part 1: Arriving

Bratislava

can I write about a city I've merely
visited? — several times, mind you:
I know this view from Martinus's
second-floor window seat
tram #8 Ružinov rumbles below
while the thin waiter bends forward
with my latte and practises his English
asks what I'm reading, seems
less keen to hear how I answer, but

his kindness in dropping a word
in a friendly way to a foreigner
adds a glow to his blue-black hair
which stands stiffly above his head
a kind of marvel he himself
hardly notices, so much style
we could be in Italy or up
the Danube in the Café Mozart

still... can I dare to suggest
I know some quality in him
or in those who live here next to
such worrisome anger to the east
where those in brown uniforms
pour out xenophobia and frustration
often unheeded until too late?
— but wait, I'm no prophet

and I believe that the brutalist statuary
from a former regime after a previous war
does not touch too deeply inside
those I know who laugh here

and work hard, who harken back to
villages they came from and return to
the balm of sheep bleating, the shiny
crabapples, plums for liquor
useful in loosening thought

and that I may have found a place
I can talk about, not like it's home
but where a few words of the graffiti
omnipresent in the capital become clear
in the usual curses, nothing about
the man I see who skips nimbly
off the tram to avoid the ticket collector
and then springs back aboard
the moment it's safe to ride free

'DO YOU SPEAK RUSSIAN?'

I asked the tall man, blue eyes
of a Slav, when in Sweet Art Café
with its strong coffee here in North Van
I heard him amid the hubbub, and
his timbre conjured a prairie friend
whose parents declaimed poems in Russian
and who himself often recited at my request
that I might hear in his voice
how a deeper life speaks out

so already inclined to this stranger
whom I approached and spoke to
surprising myself but maybe not him
(had he come here to learn English
and there I was already enunciating?)
when he pointed to the empty chair
I set my Americano next to his

I was wrong about the language
and now when I visit Bratislava
I begin to own the few phrases
often heard when Miro speaks:
dobre, dobre, ano, ano
good, good, yes, yes
and Russian? some architecture
presents a Soviet sternness, yes
but the local café, Zlatý Bochník
(Golden Loaf) is all Slovaks
I say cappuccino, I point at pastry
I sit and sharpen my ear
to hear beyond the hegemony
of English English every day

'funny'

Miro points to a row of second-floor windows
(on some *ulica*/street whose name escapes)
each ornate in history's way, and tells me
he spent years in those bright rooms
singing in a choir, 'a funny time,' he says
and several steps later as we cross
tram tracks, I ask, 'funny how?'
in Canada we might mean
those days were somehow oddly *off*
but he explains, 'a time without problems'
and I understand, 'a time of fun'

even small differences continue to surprise
and reveal who each of us is, what
our cultures and languages have made
like his number 1 with its slight
tilt with an added angle at the top
that risks becoming a seven, as if
haunted by a touch of the Cyrillic

and he has little use for 'I' because
when admiring a house, for example
his grammar leads him to say 'it likes me'
and so his world is animated, filled
with metaphor cheerfully directing
its attention onto him, greeting him daily
while his Canuck friend must search
in himself, object after object singled out
to find what is enlivened out there
and so misses the rush of feeling from the world
continuously coming to embrace him

14

HIS COMMUNIST PORSCHE

is what he later called the toy car
his father brought back from Düsseldorf
from a conference there in the West
where he could not take his family
wife daughter young son, a ransom
for his guaranteed return, Ernest
a shoe designer from Czechoslovakia
accompanied by a secret service man
to prevent contagion and defection
though there was no thought of that, not
with his little boy waiting for marvels:
foreign candy, chewing gum
magazines, and a tiny metal car

the child agog at perfect beauty
in his hand, to match the childhood
he would later call complete
freedom — how he could be gone from
his parents for hours and they never
worried, everyone worked and no one
needed money, the food was clean
the community alive with talking —
except that the border was closed and
what lay behind it could only be imagined
except that a knock on the night door meant
occupants had to leave immediately
as Party people heaved themselves in

his father returned, always he returned
and each time the West came with him
riding along on new smells of shiny paper
in catalogues, but mostly it came by hand:

15

the feel of the toy, its solid German
guarantee that it would outlast perhaps
the child, certainly his childhood
and even the revolution that flowed in from
Poland, which opened the border and flooded
his own son with hundreds of plastic cars
abundantly unable to produce such love

cadet M

offers this story: he's 23
just after the revolution in Czechoslovakia
in '93, he carries two official papers
to the army headquarters
one says he must join the military
the other says go to the university faculty
of physical education, and with his father
behind him, he knocks on the infantry door
a small aperture slides open, he sees
only two eyes, slips in both papers, asks
what must be done, and is told he *must*
join the army, end of question
until bluffing his way forward
cadet M mentions his lawyer
and in a moment the door opens

he sees a fat man
who reads both papers and sends him upstairs
to a second fat man, whose name on his door
reads the same as on the first door
this man tears up the army paper
and says it's over, not wanting any further
mention of that lawyer, a new phenomenon
in a nation edging away from Communism
toward the previously unimagined

yet cadet M wants more: incontrovertible proof
a letter to liberate him from the army, he insists
but is told they have no secretaries
so he asks for a typewriter, the heavy machine
is hauled out and he types the letter

that guarantees his liberty, signed
and stamped by the second major

and all the while cadet M's father cries
he cannot imagine acting against the state
in this way, in awe — *bázeň!* — of his son's
desire for freedom and the power
of his reach toward a future
of his own making

Freedom

though what do I know about it
I who was never held at a border
even as I pass through remains
of a crossing — Vienna to Bratislava
driven by Miro and his young son
gate poles rusting, broken glass
abandoned doors forever open
where military men once stood

I hear of his first journey with a friend
after the Wall fell: both nineteen
and allowed into the unsettling
abundance of Mariahilfer Straße
with its Viennese mannequins

freedom ever after ranked
first of requirements:
to travel in the world
passing matter-of-factly
through boundaries

I can hear how he speaks
of being free
that I might join
with those who rejoice
speeding past fallen
former state structures
while from afar
in some ways I can't see
(while he can) I bring
my culture in me

how it opens for friends
the expanse a heart can make

VÝCHOD

we are underground in
the operný parking when I learn
east in Slovak is also exit:
východ the sign says, and I try
to repeat my friend's pronunciation
and fail and try again, and fail
but, oh, that in Communist times
east with its meaning 'the way out of here'
led to deeper Soviet confinement!

but later when we eat in a Czech
restaurant near the never-stopping
Danube and drink Pilsner Urquell
I hear of the pre-lapsarian
qualities of that era: no fears
for the safety of children
no worries about medicine, no crime
no guns except in the army, not everything
about money, no non-productive seniors subsisting
on a pension of 300 euros a month

yet the border was closed, contained
a kind of paradise in a cage
until opened, when in flowed...
but we need not parade these ubiquitous ills
so I ask, 'was it worth it, that portal?'
'but of course,' he says
'people all around the world
must meet'

I cross a Border into a Faraway Land

about which we know nothing
so said Britain in 1938
leaving Czechs and Slovaks to meet bravely
the Luftwaffe, the soldiers gallant
but ill-equipped, and today

I walk Bratislava's old streets beside
the progeny of those defeated, subjected
killed, mocked, maimed, denied
I breathe the air in their city
and in their mountains, beside their Danube
while history shifts, breaking necks
in one place, putting pillows in another
I ask for translations of the city's graffiti
imagine what *I* might have written
during its wars had I been born under
those stars, without the barrier of years

though when I drink wine with friends
the smallest of hopes grows
despite the stars sending down beams
to tell us how alone we are or perhaps
how much better we can be if only...
my imagination stalls, unable
to grasp the oncoming, I reach instead
for *frankovka modrá*, dark Slovak wine
so this shared moment at least can shine

prešporák

on a street with stones that cause my feet
to twist, with graffiti-fed walls
that lean in as they rise to the gold
and green steeple above Michael's Gate
a one-room café serves coffee from Rwanda
or an elderflower and thyme concoction
that liberates the tongue into summer

surrounded by old books, students
talk *hovädiny*, or so Miro says, trash
I understand nothing they say though
they laugh and carry on, unconstrained
I remember my own carefree
college days when I discovered
poetry could be mine and perhaps
philosophy except Kant's door never did
open the way Dr. Owen claimed it would

the menu's tattered and stained
with charm, fingered, considered and
spilled upon by Slovak coffee-lovers
as they turn toward one another
to whisper little words that grow large
while all the doodads listen in: dusty
typewriter, telescope aimed up,
an unlocked bird cage, a model ship
setting sail by the cake display, windows
open to the narrow street, light falling off
medieval walls, no rhetoric
only time apparently stalled
as if to allow friendships
to stream as easily as daylight in June

even if outside and not far away
apartment blocks of Communist architecture
pile up on one another, concrete on concrete
with little grace and less sunlight, to remind us
that even amid the simple connections
men by casual chat co-create
through caffeine, a shadow may fall
and block one mind from another
so we will require all our thoughts like beams
to break the man-made stoniness and yield
a softer, longer line of beauty

Mileтičоva Market

that autumn day we walked to the market
whose name I could not pronounce
trying to make my lips and tongue
soften into Slovak, to slide off a little

what could be the point of remembering
a flavour that came off greasy paper
biting into hot dough held up by
two fingers, flatbread otherwise called

a name I can't recall — yet much else
returns: the crowd of locals looking tough
or less privileged than I felt, their rough
clothes, circle of fat men drinking at noon

one thin man bending to listen, his cigarette
angled down, a patient girl with purple
barrettes waiting as her mother searched
inside her purse; buckets of sauerkraut

peppers, lavender, children running
among legs while I at one booth
bought a cap, brown corduroy
green clouds of dill watching...

is it possible to go back, to when
I was made new because I saw the new
where my friends had often shopped?
they knew me well enough to know

I would find among the vegetables
and the offerings a taste for local life
that can enter a traveller and live
longer than memory, more lasting

the way garlic on the tongue lingers
and meanwhile inside you cleans
your liver, gives you that second chance
to enter the mélange of feelings

tenisový zápas

tennis match
in a local arena — we walk there
my friend and his father, one
younger than I am, one older
we step out from the apartment
skirt the city lake, wear layers
because the cool breath
of night is coming

yet light still fills the sky
rises up from water, I take
their photograph, arrange
dark bark of a mature tree
gold leaves bright behind them
friend rests his right arm
on his elder's shoulder, almost
an embrace, the father's hands
stuck in jacket pockets
a natural pose but both still stiff
so I joke, and smiles deepen

I think now of that exhibition game
between two spry former top seeds
their intense faces on billboards
and try to recall what I said
that made my companions laugh
maybe just *tenisový zápas*
for even the most polite
cannot always keep mirth
from erupting
when I speak, my mouth
filled with too much or not enough

the twist of lips not mastered
not even approached
nowhere near the ease of nuance
between father and son
the said and the unsaid

Irony in Bratislava

for Damian

Slavín: the monumental war memorial
remembers Red Army men and women
who now reside in mass graves covered
serenely by grass I dare not walk upon
and below the star, in the violence of stone
rifles in arms, agonized faces endlessly
agonizing, never to find a personal peace
in dying, which we honour by being here

alive, what oaths these soldiers would utter!
the embassies and BMWs, well-kept walks
where a local matronly actress, so sure
we'd recognize her, smiles her famous smile
while sweethearts bend towards one another's
need, this path best for its expanse
their wispy apparel far from the stink
worn by city saviours deafened by guns

Damian points out excitedly the moment
the lights of Slavín brighten the night
skyline, a distant jewelled finger
pointing up, atop which one
grey soldier continuously unfurls a flag
that does not waver, fiercely steady
whether the wind blows east or west

HOME VIDEO

we watch the minutes-old baby boy
squirm, the brusque nurse unwrapping
him, leaving behind a white blanket
tinged with blood and vernix, his leg
straightened for measuring, his earthly
weight registered on metallic scales
a tube stuck into him, and snot
or its pre-birth equivalent sucked out
not a loss like the loss of the womb

he is placed then on his mother's breast
while his father continues behind the lens
his hand steady – and we who watch
these ten years later recognize
in that little monk's face the mouth
that belongs to the boy with us
here on the floor, not quite sure how he
has already travelled such a distance

he is given his name, his fontanel
closes so the cosmos can no longer
stream in its messages, and as if
to compensate for this second loss
his parents love him and each other
the more, this multiplication of love
almost shocking them with its intensity
and now his audience admires how he sits
in his stroller, then sees his father dip him
in the Adriatic, swishing the little nude boy
among the salty waves while his mother
under the umbrella reads and rests

thus the days continue as they must
and we remark upon them, feel our own
trajectories and believe the boy has landed
in this living room so we might learn
from his way of being, his first words Slovak
his food and playmates, his cousins
Slovak, but his father intends him to gain
all the world, and helpless to explain
he reaches now to ruffle his son's
thick hair, his own already thin

čučoгіеɒка

'blueberry,' or 'apple,' *jablko*
not examples of pie in the sky
i.e., aspirations, I explained
beyond natural capability
both of us more interested

in choices we might make
with our mouths – I thought
of my mother's raisin creation
brimming with dark sugar
and a crust of rising gold

I chomped through thoughtlessly
presuming everywhere
had such fare, surely not
a rare great expectation
from a naïve boy's point of view

(even if famine in China
came in waves back then)
and prompted by time I asked
Miro for his impromptu sky-
target – a ticket to Bhutan! –

we both looked up as if to see
hovering in the heavens more
than sun, then instantly loved
its vastness we could not live
without, food for our light within

dusa

means 'soul' in Slovak, he said
then went on — but wait
was he saying *dusa*
also meant 'rubber'? on a bicycle?
the one he pointed to

propped outside, a black tire
that touches metal and earth
and makes a line, that
achievement we understood
tracks in dust or mud

a kid's joy in wheeling
through air that brushed
ruddy cheeks, shirt flaps
flying — while over coffee
with its speedy fluid

I turned my ear this way
and that to catch what
I'd not considered before
at first a whisper, then more
arriving with force, surprise

and so we laughed at words
each one a little guru
so sure of its ability
to command attention
we so willingly gave

HOVÄDINY

means 'not important' in Slovak
but as the word emerged in greater
context I heard it come closer
to BS, the way Miro tossed it
as we entered and left a store

a Bratislava citizen, he attempted
to tune my friends' ears and mine
to the soft 'l' we could barely
hear, certainly not pronounce
just as he had trouble with the 'v'

in Vancouver, which he managed
beautifully by the time his four months
ended and he flew home, leaving us
to wonder what else besides the
softness of a consonant we had missed

his self-containment we understood,
a sportsman's, blue-eyed focus
and the way old houses brought him
joy and awakened his village within —
a world before money

which rekindled my own child-self
climbing without fear into a wagon
to sit between two strange men
horses waddling ahead, tender
joking I understood as kindness

Hviezda

means 'star' in Slovak, and
that evening we thought
at first Venus was a plane
landing at YVR except
it didn't move, just brightened

above the city, the sky
behind deepening into black
Miro cooking his country's
famous *kapustnica* soup
and when we ate our fill

I looked into the night sky
and heard myself wonder
that I might have been born
elsewhere, hours of air travel
away, perhaps where paprika

grew in a garden and wise
hands grated cabbage
into sauerkraut and added
salt and blessings – or where
men rode in war machines

stars on their shoulders –
instead, fortune found me
in good company, half-dozing
(*driemajúci*) and distance
no more than a table length

LÁSKAVOSŤ

I said to Miro, to practise
pronouncing 'favour' in Slovak
which also means kindness!
my head tilting at their linking
as if I'd misheard

then leaving favour behind
I leapt on to nuance instead
eager to explain that
yes, he was kind to his mother
but he was not her kindness

unless of course truly he was!
he the part in her that let her
love the world so that she left
cruelty behind when he was born
an only son, always a favour

from the gods few believed even
lived anymore, how at the instant
of their demise they kindly
discharged us before they themselves
dissolved: vapour, steam, heat rising

vanished, only present now
when a mother made soup
filled the house with vegetable
smells, the tug, animal:
umbilical, primal and always kind

Part 2: Staying

LESSONS FROM THE SCHOOL OF TIME

stará škola, she said, old school
what we were discussing
I immediately forgot, drawn
into her way of relaxing
even with her phone screen smashed
our first meeting at Waves
Coffee in North Van rain

oh, other trips followed,
her here, me there, photos on phones
holidays overlapping, but this time
stays clear: Susan uses Google
to translate her words and speak
to me, her husband's newfound
new world friend, he back
in Bratislava and she visiting
their daughter studying here
a week of Pacific storm
not ideal but submitting to it
like a local, noting clean forest air
as much as the deluge

she prints *stará škola* in my notebook
and speaks its delicious sound
the slant of her letters different
from Miro's on a previous page
his *nikdy nevieš*, 'you never know'
useful when I need to sound wise

in her I glimpse
children, travel, books
does she catch something of me?

words, worries, books?
our umbrellas come up as we leave,
different colours, red and black
the language of the rain
understood by both of us

were I a GOD, I WOULD THROW a THUNDERBOLT

into the lane, turn pavement
into a wide, slow river, blue as
the sky and burbling at the grassy
overhanging banks where willows lift
their leaves to reveal my perfect creations:

a father and young son fishing
leaning their rods over the water
bits of salami for bait, floats bobbing
as a fish nudges and considers,
bites, and the boy jerks up hard
to hook its mouth, then the reeling-in
the father offering his old advice from
the years when he was young, before
even that time he fell in love and white
fishes jumped from him into the warm
waiting womb, natural as now
here above the shore the prize
dangles in space, comes flopping
to earth, gasping, wanting to return, away
from sunlight on its unaccustomed eye, helpless
while the man extracts the line
and the boy slides the fish back
into the current, watches its reviving
flip and re-entry into wet made new

so as a god I am satisfied
pleasure has been achieved without
death — though violence I am unable
to forestall, and out of the river mist
I watch the high-rises re-emerge
the patched concrete and cars

with their accelerating fumes
as father and son pack up their
paraphernalia, their bond
strengthened by silence together
the journey home to their city untroubled
by the days waiting
to leap and be borne

we sHare TaBLes anD LauGHTer

without strain, friends and something more
the way we take care of each other
aware of how the boy likes a corner
by the sofa to gather his books, water bottles
phone charger, and on my grandmother's
rickety table he lays out Canadian coins
old lottery tickets, candy, drawings
a casual creation out of himself
this child beloved by us all but
needing to have his way at not always
the best of times, and evenings he lounges
on the couch, one leg up on its back
as if to look out the window
and catch the night beyond my WiFi
that enthralls him on his cells
and keeps his mind engaged with games

his sister, their parents carry space
among the tall, dry trees, down to
the stony beach, but planks block
the remembered way so we climb
a height of bulging rock shoulder
sit searching the unreachable water below
for the sail or wave we might recognize
and grow a little apart, resting
each on our own island yet everyone near

later, wonderment at how the boy
can kick a pine cone up the street for
a dozen blocks until it falls in a drain, his
cry of disappointment at its disappearance
undercut by his elfish grin, and his father

loping ahead, his mother behind
conferring with his sister, where to eat
and what, in a foreign land, each person
me included, with ideas of dinner
sushi, Subway, fries, wine, though we
are unanimous about the blueberries

вanska štiavnica

its blue roofs with casement windows
look up to one square church tower
that crowns and maybe crows about
an old volcano, where earth opened
I step down into the hillside mine
and because I understand nothing
our guide says (except his humour)
I read the exhibits as words:
in the lurid light of underground
nearly naked men bend over tools
wear only boots and loincloths, heat
so intense at their depth

up in our cool air, in the bustle
of a holiday fair — children, actors
handcrafted knives, toys — I buy
a tiny black bell plus one postcard:
three blue windows and beneath each
three architectural Xs, embellishments
from an age needing to balance
the white flesh that laboured below

a crowd of singing young men passes by
cementing male bonds with beer
they soon vanish, the old world
returns and with it the question of
who might relish this postcard
who could dwell in time past
without hankering for its unattainables
I can't send it to myself, I know that,
already the day is ending, at coffee
I sit near lovers bending

over their cakes, eager for
nightfall and what they may find
in the heat of the dark

Hero and Leander in Bratislava

the old story is revealed to me via
five tapestries hanging in a palace
seventeenth-century English threads
hidden in the walls, discovered
during renovations, a complete set
creates the outcome of tragic love:
pale, mourning Eros peers
into the water that swept Leander
to his death, as if to find consolation
not reminders, his short bow broken

but what's a god to do when called
as he was called to draw the man
toward Hero, his beloved? whose
many-threaded features shine
with passivity as if she has seen
Eros's failure to calm the elements —
and what is love if not
what's stronger than the ordinary
day with its wind and waves?

faced with the sad end to this myth
and faced with the millions of threads
and decades of work, English
weavers going blind, centuries-old
repairs in the fabric along the edges
how easy to forget that first came love
Leander wild at the water's edge
swimming into forbidden space

DrIVInG TOWarD NITra

private anxieties arise as we travel
through countryside new to me
though these preoccupying concerns
do not emerge from the green hills
or the spires of churches that hover
above the small cities we cut through
their highway gas stops no trouble
to ignore, phrases on the neon signs
unreadable by me yet their pleasing
visuals aid my slipping into
thoughtless mind tracks that appear
as universals in anyone's life if
a lulling noise sets in, for example
when car tire hum asks how much
self-truth one can muster and maintain

this oft-repeated inner operation stops
when I notice outside a banner slung taut
between trees in a bald spot on an
approaching hillside: 'NATO get out/
Yankee go home,' slogans that spark
ire in my companions whose countrymen
have hoisted these cries in a region
that I learn leans to the right and
whose elected members expound easy
answers to complex problems in ways
that suggest history could repeat itself
here among the shadowed valleys

attentive beyond myself now, I'm aware
the words hung on the hill are English
even as they recede in the rear window

the canvas itself a borrowed thing
not entirely indigenous, which truth
relieves me a little, and before long
I am once again stirring my familiar
fretting though with some part now
newly attuned to what may yet be said
what signals may arise that would be best
for me to catch early rather than
when we can say too easily how
events were always inevitable here

I Learn Thank You

is *ďakujem,* and sorry comes second
prepáčte with its accents
like little shields held up to deflect
my attempts to speak the word
and not make Slovaks smile
they suppress their laughter
but not their surprise
at how far from or close to
right sounding I can be
as my lips flip and flap

next comes *nech sa paci*
(like English 'next Apache'
uttered quickly) – how to say
you're welcome – at a picnic table
sitting with three men, boys
sword-fighting with tent pegs,
after each toast of herb liquor
we say *na zdvarie*
and sometimes *nech sa paci*
and a severe desert fighter
tilts in to the conversation

– then from a café matron
starring in a fifties movie I learn
this greeting means 'you are here'
– she doesn't wait for my thanks
before she welcomes me
I point to her unpronounceable pastry
walnuts, cinnamon, honey, overlacing
crusts, say *prosim* – and cappuccino, too
at last a common tongue

aLeBO

the first distinct word I hear
out of the gabble of sounds
its three points delicate thumps
on a delicate drum: a-lee-bo

and hearing without understanding
I conjure a wind that foretells
the arrival of a childhood friend
one I'm forever connected to
though he's not often seen: both boys
as I create them creating themselves
fathers now with wives
and grinning upgathered kids

alebo: said always with a tone
that lifts the spine, an offering –
the story two men unwind
over coffee, a sidewalk snowy
beyond windows steamy with thought
where they say *alebo*, and I hear
an extension of an explanation
some final further extra perfect point

alebo: a kiss to the ear
almost Italian if you hear it wrong
and best heard among children
in playgrounds, never the loudest word

I ask – and learn
beauty in its simple meaning: 'or'
always ready to introduce something more

pension

with grime in the grooves
of the stove dials
one hair in the bathroom sink
a black curving signature
of incomplete care
though the sheets are brilliant
white and new, the pillows firm
mainly the room smells
too much of old wood:
bed, table, armoire all
charming on the web
and me a victim of clever lighting
and reviews by the less particular

I walk out past the college
where young Slovaks, smoking, ignore
both the orange graffiti on their walk
and me, already passing the café
hectic with day-wake, unshaven men
overhanging a tall table
a little loud, like night birds nearly spent
and no room for foreign elbows there

I carry on, make my way
to Old Town before too many more
like me arrive, find Bon Bon open,
order, and while I admire my
chocolate croissant I send messages
to the world, a morning
of hello – nothing much more –
to those in my contact list
interested in hearing what I find

even if today I will be
as imperfect as the rooms
I return to at night
grateful for the familiar
and the bookmarked novel on the bed

DOBré ráno

I leave the rented apartment
wonder who I will meet
on the common stairs
that lead me down
onto Ondavska Street
this morning, perhaps no one
just plants on the landings
old twisty geraniums here
on the next level nothing
then, one floor lower, violets
I speculate about (who decides?)
as I bounce downward
now I hear swishing
and smell water and the cleaning pail
a woman stepping back
to let me pass, the first
to mark her shiny floor, and she speaks
a long sentence without raising her voice
holds the mop handle to her bosom
in this chore which seems
no chore at all to her
her pleasantries with me the same
she'd spare for anyone – and I
do not speak, not even *dobré ráno*
'good morning,' not wanting
to jar her and set her wondering
the smile I give she returns, forgives
my untimely intrusion, maybe even
assumes I am local, after all
did I not buy this very cap
in her city's outdoor market
among the many vendors

offering familiar flowers, mushrooms?
though some root vegetables
I am not sure I could name

zajtra

part of me stays behind
in Bratislava, walks in snow
beside a city lake, no footsteps yet
to shadow the white path
but now, look: a smoking
squat man with a scowl he's been bearing
for some time, brown trousers
pushed into waterproof boots
well worn, their comfort though
does not stop him from glowering
so accustomed to how wet snow
sucks at his soles, but that is not
the source of his sourness — even so
we manage a glance at one other
though how much more I need
to grasp what has turned him
against this snow, which he scuffs,
against the grey light over the lake
after the white summer swans have flown
where he cannot go — oh, he has the euros
but no distances in his heart, what worries him
lies close to home, in his apartment
he hates the dog, maybe, that barks at night
past the hotel and near to Bajkalská
where the heavy traffic runs
the Škodas aimed at a workday
because it is morning, already tomorrow —
zajtra — where anything can still happen
so the part of me that stays behind
starts out again from Ondavska Street
as the snow falls

RUŽINOV QUIZ

I order my pastry by pointing
but some English slips out
wanting to make an appearance
in this Ružinov café, to see
and to ask: is there anything here
for me? can anyone hear me?

among clusters of habitués
a young man sits alone and alert
he's read the revolutionary
thin thumbed novels
laptop on a chair, paper in his hand
cappuccino, leather case
shirt and jeans black but
not of the kind eye-light disappears into
his black deflects all glances
yet allows him to examine
us and his new thesis there

I carry my tray, sit and stir
savour both food and sustenance
living in the air around me:
everyone is talking or listening
a threesome of businessmen
women, babies, lovers
and with elaborate writing stitched
on the backs of their jackets, workers
who glance at their phones and frown

but he looks only at me:
wants to know who am I
to have landed here with my language

he knows enough of its *S* sounds
and to pre-empt all questions I could ask
why grow your hair that long, why
keep scooping it off your forehead
and why wrap a scarf (with metallic threads)
so tightly around your neck
he could ask me to be serious, please
to answer the question
solve the quiz my presence here creates
he wouldn't mean philosophically
he'd mean: winter in a Slav suburb?
not some breezy, palm-frond beach?

but now he rises, dons
his puffy jacket, gathers up
materials, his gloves, leaves behind
his cup, steps out to Bratislava's
January sun and leaves me to suspect
any theory that makes him him —

as for his guess? let his acumen
turn kind and recognize me
as a brother *študent,* bespectacled
traveller off the tourist track
a thinker with hardly any hair
and on my face a smile that says
you can talk to me
but I may not understand

THE COUNTESS

she rather frightened us
knocking on our door demanding
to talk to me, her English clear
as she bent upon her walking stick
who was I? she wanted to know
I had heard she was too much
but I went with her next door
she had me lift down crystal glasses
for the local herbal liquor
we both laughed at our lack
of hesitation though I worried
her teeth might spurt across the divan
'it tastes of juniper,' I said
and she opened a big dictionary
to discover to our delight
I was correct, *borovicka*

photos of her husband
hung large upon the wall
white hair combed like a mat
across a sunny forehead
their grandson a russet-haired
smiler, protected by the irony
in his grandfather's grin
of the kind seen when
'the Revolution' means
the fall of Communism
and overwhelming events are not
merely private ones

she took down album after album
her son in the Dakar Rally

the expense, the dust
insurance shipping from Le Havre
and behind her a spinning wheel
covered in lamb's wool
flowers from family on the table
she could not stop telling
her stories, how twice
she lived in Prague, her husband
a composer and head of the organization
of musicians, conductors and composers

she was not a countess, such advantages
long eliminated here though
her frank stepping forward
and the plaque on the wall
spoke of more than worthiness
its brass and wood honest
her students still phoned her
apartment — larger than my host's
and she all alone with photos
apparently where we all arrive
if life is long enough
yes, on the wall, those smiles every day

I hope to see her again
pushing towards me a gilded saucer
of pale, salty peanuts
she revealed her age, but I won't
her husband had clout
she knew I knew, and she was pleased

'I am ABDUL'

a young man says as he accosts me
though accosts is not quite correct
because he's neither bold nor aggressive
even if he does ask for my attention
on this European street, his face open
so that I stop, with a tourist's curiosity
about what he expects from me
thinking perhaps he wants more
than money, but I cannot imagine
even were it true what that might be

he speaks an English I half understand
says he's not a crazy terrorist, right hand
chopping at his left wrist repeatedly
an action I assume he has seen
on TV, for surely he has not felt a blade
cut his limb, he does not look traumatized
with his winter hood pulled around his face
lips not chapped but soft and full
his parka clean, even his small yellow dog
with a leather bite guard looks well fed
and when it pulls on the leash
his master speaks patiently, aware
an animal lives in another realm

it's Munich he needs to reach
yet I don't know why, except that, yes
more money is needed if he is to attain
his goal, and so I press a two-euro coin
into his open palm, saying, 'I am David
from Canada, remember me,' just as I
will remember how his eyes light up

at the mention of my country as if there
some magic might await a man
called Abdul on his mysterious way
maybe to Munich or to somewhere closer
where two euros would fall from his hand
the very one I keep seeing constantly
chopping, urging into me a picture
intended to make me give

THIS TIME TOMIS, A MONK FROM CROATIA

sits next to me on the jet
slowly we probe one another's
character, and I learn he's the last
of eleven siblings born on a farm
that he was always a practising
Christian and then one day
after reading the gospels
he did not mind the smell
of the pigsty it was his chore to clean

his body slim, his cheeks sunken
his smile infectious, joyous
and when I overestimate his age
(perhaps an attempt to draw him closer
to my time) he laughs and says my error
doesn't matter, and in deference
to my unknowing doesn't continue
with liturgical phrasing he might
speak somewhere else, of his belief
that he will live forever

we compare our continents, fortunate
that we know a little of each other's
geography, that his English is sufficient
to manage pleasantries and complexities:
we translate 'deciduous' to *listopadan*
and think the latter more poetic

he asks about my beliefs, gently, as if
it might be a wound that needs healing
the armrest between us goes up and
does not come down for the duration

of the flight, we exchange addresses
though don't we also know when we
shake hands, step into different queues
at passport control, that we will not
meet again, unless, as he says
in heaven, a possibility just now
I do not refute, even if I consider it
one that passes all understanding

Lavender Sachets

first in the Dubrovnik market
from a giant whose blue eyes
search and insist
his flowers will last
and I believe he finds
more than a sightseer
seeking a local's blessing
I leave one in my suitcase
one in the cupboard for pillows

next in Zagreb I see
the hurried crook of a man's
shoulder blades, sun a hot shock
among citizens carrying
transacted vegetables
greens and browns, and red
his ribbon, on one sachet
not quite tight so it spills
while a second bundle haunts
a closet, the clothes there
awaiting transport to bags, bins

wizened woman in Bratislava
her smile easeful, her gesture
without grasping, affection
for passersby true, and so I buy
a bundle, go back for another
wanting some of her light
one of hers I sleep with
the other I stash in the sticky
wooden desk drawer
I rarely open – but

overcome its resistance
and I am returned at once
to her gnarled golden hands
coin aglow against deep lifelines
perfumed by purple fields

prosim

means 'please' in Slovak, pleasing
in both *pro* and *sim* sounds
the times I said please pour
yourself some *vina* or please
don't hesitate to say

slower, please, when I rushed
my sentences so that Miro
caught only every fifth word
and I pictured my speech
like a bird that flew along

touching down to the earth
once, maybe twice before it
ran out of zest and stopped
at his incomprehension
as he tried to grasp my sense

and once I said 'totally'
so speedily it sounded
like *tow-tlee*, like birdsong!
though not one heard in
Slovakia, rare even in Canada

yet those slurring two notes
he laughed away: he knew
their intention was always
to please the listening ear
to reach it with everyday ease

rozHÁDZaný

means 'rattled' in Slovak, he said
the morning he told about
springing back before a big car
ran him down, the white walk
signal untruly telling him he was safe

I said the sun must have blinded
the driver's eyes, sun so rare
and you're invisible, Miro
I joked, like all Slovaks here —
when last did we see a Slovak?

rattled, because usually traffic
here is polite, unlike his city's
where pedestrians have to cross
cautiously, cars are king
and walkers never smile

too long behind closed borders
some wary of what others say
their language owing a debt
to history, more Russian than
English available for curses

if over 30 you'd know Czech
and German and other fears
a nation the size of an island
surrounded by five larger ones
and far from the calming sea

ruka

means 'hand' in Slovak, first word
I learned because the autumn
deepened one day, Miro
and I walking up Lonsdale
I asked him to say hand

and then winter, cold —
zima, zima, starting to bite —
I attempted emphasis: roo-
ka, simple two-beat thumps
found in my mother's womb —

no verbs and their queasy
actions — just as he asked for
fog, cloud, toque, mist
and we both laughed at
nos stava, nose juice

wipe it away with your *ruka*
the firm sound of it
hand of a woodcutter, home
from the forest, now stirring
soup with a fairy-tale spoon

first times we shared coffee
at the cafés, we shook hands
— Europeans often do —
and then we stopped, arriving
instead at words: *slova*

smutný

means 'sad' in Slovak, maybe
homesick — everyone knows
how the struck chest sags
how the twist in the valves
yields an arid song

we must turn our faces
away from friends when
such feeling builds, fearing
kindness will trigger
the uprush of tears

when asked, 'what gives
strength?' Miro looked away
said, 'boyhood returning
before sleep,' sweet warmth
he savoured, a nakedness

that gave for one moment
assurance to continue — and if
perturbing events prevailed
to je život — it is life — not
to diminish but to accept

that fullness extracted a price
he paid at evening
in order to arise next morning
reborn, the old *smutný* cloak
not to be worn at all that day

šťasтný

means 'happy' in Slovak but also
'lucky,' a good pairing of the near-
impossible, I said, and Miro
laughed, understanding jokes
a sign of his improving English

then he showed me how
to stretch the mouth sideways
to say the word: as one grins
with lips in a line, his language
using more mouth, less tongue

than mine – and slowly
I heard a door open
where he once had lived
amongst the days he owned
then, a boy whose father

whistled from a window
time now to come home
all the hours he played
so freely with his friends
in the gardens, on streets

I heard that door again
as we bent over sushi, a first
for him, when its freshness
made him speak of food
his mother made each day

Part 3: Leaving

overwHeLmeD

for Robin and Evicka

because newborns have arrived
a granddaughter for me, a niece
for Miro, we recall our own firstborns:
I was overwhelmed, but this word
neither he nor Dominika (now seventeen)
understands though she offers
'flooded by warm feelings,' which I admit
is correct if not complete

how to explain the relief
when the child emerges safely
all toes accounted for? but then
the first precarious days:
jaundice, nipple confusion, weight loss
plus the weeks that spread ahead
where decisions would make me
an utter adult, ready or not
they would come, and this inner farrago
rendered even more baffling
by the flashing up and flaring of a joy
never reckoned with before

Miro reaches for his Slovak-English
dictionary: do I mean *premôcť*, 'overpower'?
or *pretekať*, 'overflow'? to clarify I say
in the beginning I almost couldn't cope
but he asks, 'what is cope?'
and consulting the book again, we find at last
the verb *utiahnuť*, 'to tighten'

which may carry a truer nuance
that initial trepidation like a noose
even though the birth soon loosened
what, without saying, we each know
as gratitude, *vďačnosť*, a silent companion
who stays with us every day, always close
like a daughter, like a friend
new found, new born

'SPEAK OF THE DEVIL'

I said, and Miro understood
said *hovorit o čertovi* back to me
his example classic: talking about
certain person X who just then
enters the room although

no horns on him, no black cape
flowing back into searing flames
no fork ready to pierce us even
though we're not really believers in
this fellow or his angelic counterpart

later, on the street, we meet
a deranged man, and I hear
my own mind thinking heedlessly
'the devil take the hindmost'
but I intend the local madman
no further harm or worsening run

don't mention this thought
as we walk, deem it puzzling
and worthless, until I think
is this not the way the devil
works, squeezing himself in

wherever he can? I laugh then
and feel I am learning to speak
as if I have never quite spoken before
so trusting of words to carry me
beyond any devil, towards my friend

ESL

for Laura

my own daughter laughs
because I'm speaking ESL again
Hello How Are You
me in Slovakia, she in Canada
her younger boy at the bottom of the screen
asking where's Papa
I speed up my tongue
slur and slide across
sentences to these two native English speakers
listening to a native speaker
we never think of ourselves as

that self comes alive
with my Stropkovská Street friends
whose son translates with such glee
to his grandmother
what I say in greeting her
we all agree he must be right
they share a joke
and I don't grasp
even a nuance – but to feel
such laughter lift!
erupting from ordinary happiness –
their smiles like those back home
here thrown to a city lake
from a third floor and
there onto a green hedge

panska jazda in donovaly

four of us one weekend
Miro, his son and another friend
and I the oldest, though
do I feel the wisest? not
among such attentive hearts
who know what I am still learning
about listening, speaking in English
but sometimes (they only)
in Slovak's soft and speedy tongue

his first translation
'men travelling,' though a woman friend
had suggested 'bachelor party'
but she's not here in the wooded countryside
we saunter through, the son
on his silver scooter, to take photos
of who we are when connected
to one another, to mountain air
the coloured leaves, their yellows
alive with light

later we stop at a spa, soak
and shower, cast off aches
and even catch time
as it cavorts by: the boy measures
how long we three men
spend in the mint steam room
(under 12s not permitted)
where we talk and sweat
and before leaving estimate
17 minutes, but the lad, accurate
patient with numbers, says 21

and the happily corrected
recall how once far in their pasts
and where he yet lives
seconds, hours, days
were never separate

Driving country roads in Slovakia

father and son up front joke
in language I can't follow
while the radio alternates between Jagger
and Vivaldi, and so we pass harvested fields
and roadside shrines to the suffering
crucified Christ with fresh plastic flowers
then hilltop castle ruins, goldenrod and lupine
ageless in their wild places
though their names here slip off my tongue
and dip away like the swallows
bobbing out of the creeks

then a derelict factory raises
its Communist brick chimney to mark
the passage of time, while Roma men
stand still on the roadside
tilting baskets toward us
mushrooms, blueberries for sale
as we breeze by

and now my driving friend points out
the steel factory celebrating sixty years
of making, and I catch as well
the steeple of a church
its Russian letters advertising
future space in the cemeteries we only
glance at, at the moderate speed
we've adopted for sliding through
one village and then another
satellite dishes aimed west
clouds of busybody flower-faces flowing
off the balconies, geraniums stiff and watchful

among people who rarely smile in public

it's easy to be comfortable here
on Dunajská, they talk across tables
over children's heads, I hear rhythms
that carry them along, no one caring
this foreigner knows only a few words —
beer, thanks — he comes from far away
his ignorance like openness
impossible to include in the rapid
this-then-that of chatter

I gauge my experience, guessing
what's around and in me
at a sidewalk table taking stock
the soup spoon to my lips
a teenaged couple huddles
over a phone, easy to tell they know
life is elsewhere, they look at me
once only, enough to see
I am old and alien like their parents
who have never understood

when there appears before me
on his silver scooter: Damian!
surprised to see me here, happy
to chat in English at that miracle
age of twelve when a boy is free
to travel the streets on his own
back from the school he enjoys
his parents confident he's savvy
and safe in their city — and when asked
if he wants to join me, he politely

declines, knowing Babka's baking
awaits his sweet tooth at home

a summer story of water and earth

once more I fly across the landmass
of Canada, above the Atlantic
to Vienna, take the train over leaf-green fields
where blue sky finds itself
in rivers, arrive in Bratislava
and hear my name called by a boy
who runs toward me, his smile
the sun under which I will grow
in the days with his father and grandfather

we drive to the Adriatic
where we walk along its edge
tramping on white stones
the sandals of Roman legionnaires
once felt, let the glitter
of sun on waves enter us, so nothing
needs saying, nothing that the water
and then land perfumed with
mint and dust have not already said

in the harshest heat of the day
we retreat into the shade of trees
doze and later dive again into waves
that will continue after we're gone
a consoling knowledge Earth
sends every day, just as
thinking of this boy
shining on our earth
makes old men happy
to follow his eagerness
along the path to the beach

my slovak friends

invite me on their August drive
from Bratislava twelve hours to the Adriatic
where red, yellow, green towels
drape from balconies (semaphores
of salty pleasures) and old men
blackened by heat and history
crowd wooden benches and scowl
not one with dark glasses, each
facing the glare of a Balkan sun
as if it were nothing more
than an acquaintance

my friends and I deepen our time together
walking a cliff path edged with whitecaps
and aquamarine toward a haven
where small stones press on our feet
and we lie speechless as lizards
skin darkening, until waves invite us in
or light fails and we gather
ourselves up like wet towels
and return through the buzz of cicadas
to our temporary home

later, travelling away from the sea, I learn
at a highway stop with iffy WiFi
that a friend has died, one who once
held me honestly, and I know again
how each loss matters the most, now
as we pass dry pine hills in Croatia
below distant leafless peaks
from which a soul might be launched

into constellations of white abundance
we call clouds

PASSING DOWN THE WHISTLE

my friend lies on rounded beach stones
his white-haired father stretches out nearby
while the boy bobs in waves
three generations on one strand
alike in their pleasure though histories differ:
the adults lived in Communist times
and share memories the bounding boy
will only hear as stories of an era
when travel to this shore was blocked

Miro whistles now, a sound
to pierce the air around his son
who raises his head, acknowledges
his father's admonition to come back
closer to our colourful towels
lotions, discarded clothes, lolling bodies

the grandfather hears his son's whistle
and surely he recalls how often
he whistled home this very son
to their block in Partizánske
with this same note, how it rings out
an arrow of love and intention
above the susurrus of stones
rattling back after the white wave
reverses and recedes — how the man's ardour
passed to his wife
how their child
learned to whistle
from his dad, that signature sweetness
Dedo listens to now, no doubt admiring

his son's technique, his grandson's
willing, easy obedience

I on my own stones
feel all these blood ties
and while they are not mine
a father's call to his child strengthens
what would otherwise float away unheard

SINGING SLOVAK FOLK SONGS

you cannot be shy when you are singing
when lungs fill and then release
the singer thinks not of himself
but of the outrush of heartiness

Miro turns up the car CD
his larynx and lips
shape to meet the artist's tenor
and become one sound
wilder than expected – I am carried
to plains before cities arose on them
ululating emanations from *cimbal* and *fujara*
made to resonate and buoy a voice upward
impossible to contain
in the chest – though I am unschooled
and self-conscious and can only hum and tap

I hear how he stepped out for bread one day
a student, saw an invitation to audition
sang two songs a cappella, and became
second baritone in the Lúènica Chór
which toured Europe when travel
was bound by iron borders

he recalls his mother singing
while she laundered in the basement
of their block – no other songsters
in his family? did he receive
talent and gene from some long-forgotten
tall blue-eyed warrior arrived in these hills
we now traverse? my companion
smiles, unleashes a haunting reverberation

THE WAVES AT KOŠARISKÁ

ride through the grain field
pushed by the wind
and we watchers sit
at the point of perspective
that sends the slope
upland to a hilly wood
where wild pigs live...

next door, a Rom's
tidy barn is hung with
shiny leather and ladders
his chickens wary
heads up as much as down

I have returned in time
to myth still alive
its pulse reminding me
I once was a boy

here in our chairs
we gaze upon
waves in the green wheat
soft swells that press
and then release
a snaking effect
or a boar running hotly
through the stalks
towards us, tusks up

this small thrill
ripples through me
while other joys linger:

the early morning
call of the rooster
the delicious duck at dinner
voices from the kitchen
in another tongue
the soccer ball singing
its score across the lawn
grass so much like
what I felt under knees
after landing in my first home
having arrived from a far place
and carrying still
its undulating ease

In a slovak village

it is morning, and as my sleeping companions
begin to stir, I look out at bright woods
and remember how last night
when Cricket was louder than Owl
my friend and his young son curved
under a duvet as if needing comfort
or familiar weight, despite the heat —
but soon they stretch, legs appear
their faces alike in sleep though awake
they are only themselves

through our window the village enters
Rooster first to announce that time
has moved and we must pay attention
lest we fall behind ourselves, then Small Dog's
barking punctuates and punctuates until
Sheep's bell suggests we are all one crowd
but Goose agrees it is time for alarm
to warn that we must step into each hour
intentionally or fail to belong anywhere
near plums that swell into dusty blue

in the room below us conversation
hops across Cheese, Bread and Tea
now that Moth retires to his curtain
and Fly calls his *kamarátski* troops
to begin their business of defilement
all hairy legs at the ready
and while we talk of our day ahead
Hawk's shadow falls fast upon us
and we pause, almost praying
during his plunge to summer grass

MOSCOW TO CAIRO

is the flight my friend imagines
for a jet far above
I see only the speck
of machine while its white tail
slowly vanishes
into whatever might fly there
besides Russians bound for
sand and sneering camels

down here is exotic, too
this language so melodious
everyone seems set to sing
and liquor with its taste of herbs
and fire made to kill bugs
in the stomach when taken
each morning after speaking begins
to make us common people

a shared journey awakens
the links latent in us as we
stumble on new words, plum pits
in our mouths, and we see that
what an eye says cannot be said
any other way — and so
surprise travels via the iris
and its partner the smile

and up there? passengers sleep now
their dreams not of heat ahead
but of snow behind, how frost
brings quickness to feet, fur coats

never far off, near as history
until departure delivers
a last look and words muffled
or no longer needed, already said

spa, piešťany

brought here by the kindness of others
I step into the mirror pool
and my limbs grow heavy with heat
mud oozes up
between my toes and I rub it on
chest and arms, an old soft armour
entering my skin

now I am swaddled in warm blankets
and on the swelling music from above
my mother's here to see what I've become –
she smiles to see unwashed mud
on my feet and does not mind that
my body has aged as hers has not, she's
perfect in her forest green sweater
hair dark and wavy, and a jewel
upon her breast shines gold

she touches me, says I have grown
well beyond the romping, running
child, and laughing, she leaves, rising up
and I recall her crooked hands
from the time when she was my age now
how they would have taken in
the earth's heat here – and she floats away
towards the kindness of those awaiting her
out where lime trees wave with ease

THE SPA ATTENDANT

in his white uniform does not hover
but guides us with a voice no louder
than the water's murmur
towards beds where we lie down naked
on our old backs in a post-pool daze
almost without will though feeling still
his strength, his service
in the firmness with which he binds us
almost roughly yet kindly
in warm blankets so we sweat
and let poisons seep from our pores

how many groins has he looked down at
and how might he categorize them in their
soft and shrivelled states, but surely such
notions long ago slipped from his thinking –
and after hours of listening to the music
falling from above and to the water's
quiet talking as it runs in channels and along
the limbs of those who come here to heal
does a moment arrive when loathing for
their bodies rises in him even as the smell of
sulphur wafts past? and is there then a second
revelation when self-loathing grips with
such surprise that he must turn away from
flesh altogether, his round face grimacing?

and later, when he returns home to his wife
and children, perhaps he sees in them the weight
that has tied him to work he now cannot
change, his years such that this unfolding
is the only possible one and extends even into

night dreams when he wraps up men
who are corpses, grey skin no longer touched by
the waters of life, Lethe-bound instead
and no resurrection possible except what
the attendant brings to them, his task
he relearns each day, that of breathing
into the dead a love greater than human
weakness so they may rise and walk again

Fever HOTEL

my throat aflame, my body burning
I walk into the vaulted, empty foyer
take the key up wide stairs and discover
a common entryway to adjoining rooms
each with three beds: a sports hotel
built to accommodate Soviet athletes
enough space for several muscled men
in the shower tiled floor to ceiling
with orange squares from an era
when function overrode aesthetics

I sleep while outside construction cranes
loom motionless above floodlights
creating darkness in a no man's land of
half-made, windowless structures staring
blankly at one another, waiting for a tomorrow
in which I dream a sky-high dog orbits
in a steel apparatus, spiky antennas beeping

I sweat and wake alone, I alone booked
in this place where a notice in large type
warns me to lock all doors, to secure myself
against the tide of time, to curl under
the white comforter, to listen for *something*
for silence from the pre-remote TV
but now an inner door creaks and groans
in a black and white film though the brown
shag carpet would not show the blood
that seeps from me in my fever-dreaming

later, leaving, I see a bundle of linen clumped
by an open door, though only my movement

activates the hallway light, and still I see
no one, hear no one — I have crossed a barrier
into a time before, whose tectonics
still linger, its glories gone, except for
the darting woman at the desk
who eagerly calls for my cab, keenly aware
I do not belong here and must be taken away

Roma music

1. IN THE PLAZA

in a big red chair in Ružinov
I read an American novel of lust and power
characters with names of a certain
echelon — Vivian, Travis — when I hear
two accordions, at first faint
and from this sixth floor I see
a man and a woman walk in the plaza below
sending urgent sounds to those above —
he in black sweatpants and brilliant white cap
she in red blouse, embroidered jeans, his
instrument smaller, hers played with more vigour

I lean out to hear them better
and the man, who has been looking up
spots me, waves, I wave back
and when he speaks words I don't understand
and I shout down that I only know English
he replies with 'money, money'
I throw out two silver and gold coins
watch them fall, one larger, heavier
though they will land at the same time
and as they spin and flash
I am dropping with them
now a man in a suit enters the plaza
pointedly ignoring this entreating music
and by the time I close the window, they are gone

2. IN ME

I return to my red chair with
the Roma music resonating in me —
unchanged, the novel continues its entanglements
and I wish now for some swarthy splash in these familiar
pale, languid, new world lives, an evident wildness
beyond the customary ache in heart and groin

perhaps I will yet turn a page and read
of a plan for a way I can throw myself
beyond all I am and create a music
that will cause others to cheer and to offer
a little largesse, tossed with pleasure

BaLCONY, BraTISLava summer NIGHT

I'm learning Slovak swear words
I asked to hear them
they're part of us, too

I forget all but the worst
easy to remember the worst
so bad it can't be said

I was asked, urged
never to write the word
or say it on the street

they laugh when I say it
my accent and tone
the way I embrace its violence

but this word is a curse
you spit out with hate in your heart
nothing I feel in this city

new lights on the horizon
since my last visit
European energy visible

on this balcony filled
with language, the brightest light
streaming out from this home

I pass under an archway with statues

of soot-coloured cement, two grim men
from a former time, their time to be revered
over, now we're all in a hurry to understand
our placement on history's page, and I'm
keeping in mind everyone I know here
is honest, hard-working, with an eye
to the promised betterment ahead even
as the stones under their feet and mine
remind us of sights we would
turn away from yet never forget

still, I wonder who named this street
Dunajská and who went here before –
centuries earlier I would have heard
German, Hungarian, some Slovak
or Czech, no English, they would come
later, like the Russians, the tanks and smoke
the Nazis before them: this lineage can't
be kept straight all the time

optimism abounds among the young
I have seen their faces, and when I'm lost
I halt a young woman (Europe with
cheekbones and blue eyes) who's willing
to try out English grammar and direct me
toward the tram I need, she's amused
that I'm confused, not at all wary
not the way her parents would have felt
when Communists flipped themselves into
Capitalists, stole the factories, left the workers
without support and little money for goods
not like her grandparents who weathered

wars, invaders, she can't be holding
all those stories all day long, and she
laughs when I ask her, 'can you help me?'

monastery ruin in Bratislava

at night, in night's half-light
abandoned inner yard, windows in rows
no glass to reflect, all dark, soft, stark
rubble at our feet, near the grave bones
of the men who once lived here

we feel the invitation to go walking
with ghosts, the stony corridors
stone walls and stone steps
I am mindful about where
I place my foot, on an edge or
a smooth moment that might slip

we're welcomed into a bar newly
open in one part of the ruin
its ceiling arches above us
angel wings, at that imagined angle
that once watched over men of God
and in the tradition called chalking
the door, white marks on a dark wall
C M B, the three wise men, kings
bless this dwelling each year
dates and crosses recorded there
and we remember Melchior and
Balthazar... C refuses to incarnate
until the owner, a young man
with honest face, casual manner
brings us clear liquor and spicy
onions, and we're told of Caspar

now we walk again into the night
that fails to illuminate a church,

shoulders that have rubbed the walls
the passageway narrow, centuries
of shoulders
         and of the prayers said
in all the layers of time, some stay
they come back to us from the stones
wordless, then go their own way

BOTH PRIMITIVE AND CIVILIZED, THAT'S US

off a trail near the Danube
we pick young and tender leaves
of wild garlic for chopping up
spreading later on thick buttered slices
of homemade bread eaten with
the relish of hungry hunters
who have found in their forest
what nourishes and requires
only bending down and a clear eye
because no one wants a leaf spotted
with white bird droppings though
I suggest its minerals might add
to the pungent spice, the earthy taste of
plants so abundant they form a carpet
a pauper might roll on with glee

who among us feels most deeply this moment
in this weekend, in this spring month
in this particular year? since last we met
circumstances have changed us – our work
our bodies, the unruly futures – the usual
markers of time that settle in our bones
often so slowly we do not notice
they create new parts of our stories
not yet at the denouement for those
all younger than I, I who admire how
they crouch among wild growth, rising
from green without a groan, whereas

I am best at standing and holding the bag
into which the pickers deposit their finds
while I defer to their local knowing

of this quiet wooded place by the river
with its furious forwardness and where
before we depart some of us sit briefly
on big stones that waves have pushed up here
though hardly big enough for our thoughts

IT IS Dawn Here In Donovaly

and I am always happiest when I see
the first of morning light outlined
behind a horizon of dark conifers
motionless on the hills...

just above the peaks of the trees
colour begins first, an opalescent
rose tint that never deepens
but with time
vanishes into the paler tones above
which in turn give way
to the triumphant turquoise
of the zenith

so different from sunset when light sinks
and colours become indistinguishable
from lack of light, from darkness itself...

in this dawning the colours are removed
by the arrival of light so that gradually
I become aware of what is illuminated
rather than of the light itself:

the trees return
some becoming individuals
I am almost surprised to see
I am relieved that they, too
have outlasted the night, unfazed
and again ready to stake a claim
against the hours

DEVÍN CASTLE

a ruin above the confluence of
the clear Morava with the deeper
darker Danube it fails to influence
and where men watched from heights
while water flowed past and past
endless in the possibilities of seasons
and terrors but also hours when
a guardsman's attention drifted toward
his night meal of meat, nuts or soup
while the wind blew his way,
the smells of mud and freshets spilling
near fresh burial mounds

and as he fingered his iron weapons
one slipped from his animal belt
to appear much later among amber
in an exhibit around which students
cluster, perhaps one of them aware
how time has thrown him up here
among his smoking, joking peers
to speak Slovak, to wear jeans
to find his body a mystery he worries
may never be easily understood

under my hand the cold rock that forms
this wall is solid, but I know better:
Miro takes my photo, which becomes
a *memento mori* when days from now
I discover it has remained unchanged
in my camera – still the same squint
the grey sky behind showing no sign

of Perun, god of lightning and thunder —
whereas this very hand is less

the sure thing, and yet it serves still
to crumble more stone
into the river below as I reach out
to my friend's hand and climb down from
the bastion — and so we return to our own
sensibilities, heartened here among
scrambling teens ablaze, the beauty of
a summer evening before them
sunlight slanting into warm gold
just at that moment when it sinks —
which I might notice more than they

kamzík

a communications tower that on a clear day
looks into Austria, Hungary, the Czech Republic
from up here I survey Bratislava
breathe such clean air, recall flowers
that tremble in the forest sunshine
and forget about that staring couple
below, how they smoked and scowled
watching me as if I were the attraction
perhaps because I spoke a language
that sounded unmelodic to them, unable
themselves to roll English words just as I
cannot vibrate my tongue in Slovak

and where is the tongue in English
and not in Slovak? questions
that had never occurred to me
though now I hear the clicking and clacking
of consonants as they fall on my slanted ear
and sometimes are not heard at all though
I am a willing student, so today I think
I might speak more easily with the white
flowers on the trail down from the tower
than to that twosome, sepals and petals
might open at my words, as willing to hear
as I am charmed to know them

what a bounty that man and woman
might have shared with me:
we could point to the white flower
and say its name, each in our own
tongue, the way we could laugh
at the strangeness as it leaves our mouths

when we attempt the foreign word
and the smiles that linger even after
we have parted, especially if we have
shaken hands and agreed without words
that our worth is stronger than words

and yet, and yet, to someone who sounds
as we sound, we would happily spill the story
of how we wished the light in the other's eye
had translated into a tumult of meaning
the wet taste of talk that helps us
as daily as bread, human as breath

UFO

on Tripadvisor someone calls the bridge
monstrous, but I see instead
the flying saucer shape of the restaurant
atop the span ('watch, taste, groove'
on the napkin) crowning the expanse
and there I enjoy coffee and gaze back in time
at the castle with its square ramparts
where kings were crowned for
five hundred years before the idea of kings
fell under cars and the need for transit

next I walk below the thunder of its traffic
see in historical photos how
the bridge was built: the old houses
smashed by the wrecking machines
the officials in their heavy overcoats
unsmiling at the past as it vanished
into rubble carted away, the new world
arriving on guy wires that held then
and hold now their modern vibrations

I look at the Danube below and adopt
its stance of moving on and not
allowing itself to be caught in history
not too much — also, doesn't Miro
drive over this river and bridge
almost daily? his traversing making it more
mere background: the daily we pass through
on the way to somewhere

though maybe those old Communists
who engineered this crossing

felt energy lift them into an exactitude
we now recall as alien and obsolete
as our cars (and we?) soon shall be
even while friendships drive us on
into the softer zones of laughter
and shared food or up to a sky-high
vision where we find its view of the city
distant, pleasing, all possible, a kingdom

on our walk along the Danube

the summer evening offers
a sunset with dark colours
and two kinds of time:
                            first, the river
sends its weight against shore
and bridge and without malice
intends to be in Budapest by morning
yet remain here in its molten
manner, its trick of staying and leaving

then, above us the castle is unmoved:
its stone knows centuries can be
square, each tower a testament to
history's way, which is stop-and-go
only the flag at its highest turret
allowed to change its design
and colours as monarchs deign

and perhaps a third time exists
in we who walk the narrow path
sometimes of packed sand
so I think we may be stepping
outside the stony past and beyond
the flowing future, and our faces
soften in their tenderness for the light
settling on us a glow, the reflection
off water when we know we can linger

but now Susan pulls from her bag a sweater
the night air a new reminder, and we hurry
onto the bridge whose steel flanks
we press our hands against, feeling the sun

captured there and still radiating heat
though it has already gone from us

SLOVAKS WEAR THEIR HISTORY AS A HEAVY COAT

or as a shawl, breezily, or even not at all,
free to disown the bloodshed and errors
made by ancestors — surely unendurable
any other way — and I see the spirit
the young manage here: to stay uncrushed
by the weight of tyrants and betrayers, tanks
in the street, Brezhnev in Bratislava

I see more: these men, women embrace
impending and present freedoms even if
the past has a hand on their shoulder
gripping fingers reminding with
a pressure that never entirely
ceases, and still, still, many act honourably
even with this encumbrance and so
have not been felled

I fly home to my enclave of peace,
and the history that I have swallowed *here*
slowly begins to go down my throat
though never gone from my table
and when I revisit the tribulation
I felt there, then even more
I picture my friends before I sleep
touch their heads and pray
not *to* any Unseen but *for*
their soul force to continue

and as I drift into dream I admit
to my errors of ignorance, so much
I can never know, about the trains
in the night, their cargo looking out

and to my error of arrogance
that among all peoples on earth
I or anyone is free

I am Leaving Bratislava Again

friends and familiar tables, café corners
statuary, murals, the castle rising
above a Russian restaurant's borscht
and thirteen varieties of vodka, oh
slowly the heart pulls itself away
slow as my bus leaves its lane and
merges into the stream arching over
the Danube, bound for elsewhere

around me I hear Slovak, German
English, already in the untidy world
of travellers where I keep asking
as I have often thought before
'am I leaving here for the last time?'
because a last time there must be
though can we know the moment…
so I pledge to those left behind
to stay attuned, see you soon

in summer or a season that follows
I'll push at the hour's weight, wedge
myself against its claims and climb
again into a jet and onto a bus, watch
landmarks emerge out of the horizon
ring the buzzer, shove the heavy door
ascend the stairs into old embraces
the table waiting with home-cooked
concerns: 'how was your winter?
how is your health? what is your plan?'

murder in slovakia / coffee in canada

a young journalist and his fiancée
he, shot in the chest, she in the head
and later her family buries her
in her wedding dress, far from
the grave of her husband-
never-to-be, now a corpse lowered
in his own birth village with many
weeping as well – and we who are safe
remember such news from other places
in other times, but the blood there is new

fraud, corruption, thugs, arrogance
the editorials cry out, outrage marches,
all postscripts to personal horror
that final living moment of one who saw
the red star blossom on beloved flesh
and now civic catastrophe, citizens
and their families and freedoms
feeling a hot protective pain

like that of the fiancée's mother
who, worried, called the police
who found the bodies days after death
in the village only a short drive
from the capital where later
the prime minister stacks one million euros
on a table, reward for info leading…
perhaps back to himself?

back here in North Van I ask the Czech barista
if she's heard, and she has not
and when I explain briefly

she sweeps my question away, dismissing
that country east of her interest, busy
with us, customers chatting calmly
about families, sports, pets
travel south to the sun
no future tense cold with threat
no need for our hearts to beat
with unwavering valour

airborne

on Dubrovnik's walls high above
the soft Adriatic, I see others
hesitate, grow faint and dizzy, hug
their travel companions in the heat
press their backs against stone
but none have placed pennies
in their shoes the way I have
to keep from jumping, for jumping
is the draw, the irresistible tug
already I have spread my arms
and air buoys me as I leave the wall
my descent swift but not inelegant
its ecstasy far greater than its end

in a vast Vancouver apartment
I cross the living room and step
onto the twenty-third-floor balcony
to admire the city, the blue inlet
and feel that high breeze pulling
my arms above my head, so I dive
over the railing, only waist high
a mere inconvenience to the plunge
this barrier psychological only, not
one that stops how my host gasps
as I float down, shirt flapping

on the gondola at Štrbské Pleso
I watch the earth fall away but not
so far from me to invite a leap
I enjoy the beauty of the mountain
with my friend nearby and solid
as we joyride up, skiers all around,

their equipment dangling down
we sway in the sun and wind
above tracks of animals in the snow
where the fox sees two men swinging
in the sky, neither thinking of death
though one yearns for the weight of relief
in the living seconds just before it

WILL DISTANCE EVENTUALLY OVERWHELM

and silence the goodwill generated
by technology in our phones and tablets?
each of us available but with periods
of quiet, our daily lives after all
occupy us mightily, on Lonsdale and
Dunajská, streets offering us their
histories as reminders of difference

I sat with your family in U Zlatého Bažanta
watched three gentlemen from India
in Stone Square below, white hotel
umbrellas raised, they moved slowly
close together without gestures, hatless
their sombre overcoats of the same size
and by the time our meal came and went
they seemed still unresolved as if
paralyzed by some element unknown
to us up here — and were we also
watching for you? wondering
if your meeting was over and you'd
join us and order, and what you would say
about the threesome below — it would be

kind, pithy and worth hearing
I'd ask about the distance between
Mumbai and Bratislava, compared to
the 9000 kilometres between here
where I am most days reading
musing, walking by the new café
once the old café that invited us in
to sit over coffee, and your home
where you return after patients, decisions

none of it in English, and none of
my thoughts in Slovak, yet I have
never forgotten *ďakujem* and *dovidenia*
thank you and goodbye, although
ako sa máš, how are you, is harder
to hold on to when so seldom employed

VODa

means 'water' in Slovak
for hours it fell, so familiar
I forgot to ask for 'rain'
and only later learned
dázd, like dazzle

Miro so tall he kept
the sky from dropping
I looked up to see
snowflake and fog
as he saw them here

for the first time, as he felt
the day's dawn drizzle
become bags of weather
opening, then letting out
noon-life lit by sudden sun

mostly we walked under water
falling, compared climates
and found parallels:
the promise of spring'
set us confabulating

sometimes, too, we sipped
and sat and said nothing
and — watching the rain —
heard far-off thoughts
step inside and join us

VZBĹKnuť

means 'fast burning,' 'burst
into flames' — it took weeks
to manage those six consonants
in a row, each demanding
spatial rights on my tongue

Miro asked me to picture paper
meeting match and then
vanishing into twisting flimsy
and smoke — and a memory
wafts by of a note I wrote

long ago, still think of as Verse One
— though the words penned there
I cannot recall (their bad manners
from the outset) — how I placed it
under a tent of twigs that would not

catch on its own, could not glow
in the snow that threatened me
its pressing cold all around become
a reason to believe I must sacrifice
my little verse, offer it up

— and did I already suspect the warmth
it would provide was more in the fire
at hand than in the flame I had imagined
and written? sensing there a flicker
turning fickle in its own ashen time

zaвavny

means 'funny' or 'witty' in Slovak
so when Miro read aloud our
daily horoscopes full of idioms
(phrases he called them) I snorted
at the literal senselessness of

'keep your cool!' gave up and
resorted to Google Translate
on his phone to arrive at
zostan pokjny! only he
could pronounce though I

tried valiantly before
indulging in that good laughter
born of garbled utterance
errors in tone and timbre
(hundred mistakes a day, he said)

yet sometimes my tongue
spoke truly, its twist a triumph
before the word slipped away
into the welter of admonitions
among our morning's separate

zodiac signs, each pressing
such advice from the heavens
upon us we had to smile
except when we found ourselves
inside a truthful surprise

zarezaný

means 'termination' in Slovak
and Miro drew a hand sharply
across his throat, teeth bared
impossible to miss that
slit jugular spouting

so rearing back I said, 'death!'
and grappled with *spat ako*
zarezaný, sleep as termination
his son's slumber during the week
at a beach in Croatia – ah!

spat of the dead, so deep
the child, passed arm to arm
did not stir, Adriatic waves
matching those behind
closed eyes, so his father

dropped him in one boneless
flop into bed, in awe how he
arose each morning, a blessing
at the first table of the day
milk in his bowl, family

in T-shirt, trunks, tanned feet
sand in the towels, damp
last night but ready again
for skin and salt glow to revisit
wind and its unending waves

ZLOZITY

means 'tricky' in Slovak, and
perhaps much more, for only
those who say the word easily
understand its nuances — every
language has them, those traps

of the tongue — so I repeated
the word, and if my sound
rang almost right, Miro smiled
as he knew I smiled when
he attempted tough enough

that damnable g-h of English
must have been concocted
on a bad day in Babel
(he asked, 'what is the past
of must?' and I failed there too)

all my life fiddling with words
and not penetrating them enough
to know their trappings
as I read through this list:
grave, good, god, goodie

gracious, gotcha! he wrote
hrob, dobry, boh, cukrovinka
laskavy, dostalsomta!
these he knew, like friends
without tricks, *vrelo*, warmly

zvedavy

means 'curious' in Slovak
coming to me when we rode
through the city on the bus
so many peoples having arrived
from lands farther away

than Miro's homeland, souls
living side by side with condos
so many now, like Waikiki
an incredulous local said
in awe at the pace of change

Miro's eye caught most
on wood houses, their pleasing
vernacular that spoke only
among maples and cedars
lawns and stone steps, yards

I tried to see as he saw:
new, never-before-beheld
to know as a child knows
as we talked, the rolling bus
urging the world passing by

onto us, every object we saw
shouting its word
begging us to look its way
out the window, *okno*
out the eye, *oko*

ACKNOWLEDGMENTS

Eight of these poems (some in slightly different versions, along with an interview) appeared online at *Numéro Cinq*, with thanks to Douglas Glover and Kathy Para: hovädiny; rozhádzaný; hviezda; šťastný; smutný; láskavosť; čučoriedka; 'speak of the devil'.

A small selection appeared in *Bratislava Poems* (The Alfred Gustav Press, 2018): Bratislava; irony in Bratislava; on our walk along the Danube; 'funny'; balcony, Bratislava summer night.

Five poems appeared in *EVENT 50.1:* východ; home video; his Communist Porsche; Hero and Leander in Bratislava; were I a god, I would throw a thunderbolt.

Neither Prešporák nor Sweet Art Café exists now.

Special thanks to those who read or heard various versions: Robert Adams, gillian harding-russell, Lorna McCallum, Meg Stainsby, Richard Therrien, Russell Thornton. Special thanks to Artie Goshulak.

With deep gratitude to Miroslav Dlhoš, his family and friends.

ABOUT THE AUTHOR

David Zieroth's *The Fly in Autumn* (Harbour, 2009) won the Governor General's Literary Award and was nominated for the Dorothy Livesay Poetry Prize and the Acorn-Plantos Award for People's Poetry in 2010. Zieroth also won The Dorothy Livesay Poetry Award for *How I Joined Humanity at Last* (Harbour, 1998). Other publications include *watching for life* (McGill-Queen's, 2022), *the bridge from day to night* (Harbour, 2018), *Zoo and Crowbar* (Guernica Editions, 2015), *Albrecht Dürer and me* (Harbour, 2014), *The November Optimist* (Gaspereau, 2013), *The Village of Sliding Time* (Harbour, 2006), *The Education of Mr. Whippoorwill: A Country Boyhood* (Macfarlane Walter & Ross, 2002) and *Crows Do Not Have Retirement* (Harbour, 2001). His poems have been included in the *Best Canadian Poetry* series, shortlisted for National Magazine and Relit Awards and featured on Vancouver buses three times as part of Poetry in Transit. He watches urban life from his third-floor balcony in North Vancouver, BC, where he runs The Alfred Gustav Press and produces handmade poetry chapbooks twice a year.